WORDS FROM WALLS

poems by

DM Frech

Finishing Line Press
Georgetown, Kentucky

WORDS FROM WALLS

Copyright © 2022 by DM Frech
ISBN 978-1-64662-821-6 First Edition
All rights reserved under International and Pan-American Copyright Conventions. No part of this book may be reproduced in any manner whatsoever without written permission from the publisher, except in the case of brief quotations embodied in critical articles and reviews.

ACKNOWLEDGMENTS

DM Frech has published in *Writer's Journal, The International Library of Poetry, The Poets Choice and Noble House,* also won an award in non-fiction from *Hampton Roads Writers.*

Many thanks to Finishing Line Press for publishing WORDS FROM WALLS and Jesus who woke my heart years ago and stayed, despite my protests

Publisher: Leah Huete de Maines

Editor: Christen Kincaid

Cover Photo: DM Frech in NYC East Village;
photo by Jeffrey S. Klenk, www.jeffklenk.com

Author Photo: DM Frech with sons Andrew and Samuel;
photo by Robert Frech

Interior Photos: DM Frech

Cover Design: Elizabeth Maines McCleavy

Order online: www.finishinglinepress.com
also available on amazon.com

Author inquiries and mail orders:
Finishing Line Press
PO Box 1626
Georgetown, Kentucky 40324
USA

Table of Contents

Birthday Wishes 1

Bricks 2

Darkest Corner 4

Empty 5

Empty Nest 6

For Our Time Again 7

God Broke the Silence 8

God Talks 9

Heal 10

In His Shadow 11

Jesus Said 12

Leave the Ghosts 13

My Forest Dream 14

My Heart Hears Nothing 16

My Son and Soul, Burial 17

Praises To God 18

Quagmire 19

Quiet 20

Rancour of You 21

Sleep Deprived 22

Stars Had Fallen 23

The End I 24

Thoughts of You 25

When You Are Gone 26

Words from Walls 27

You Are Heard 28

For Andrew & Samuel Frech, my sons and greatest joy who inspire me daily to leave the swamp and climb the mountain

And to my dad, Steven Kasmauski, who patiently listened to my childhood stories and songs and in his quiet way encouraged me

BIRTHDAY WISHES

Birthday wishes
to everyone who
woke up
to everyone who
didn't kill themselves
to everyone
who put one foot
forward as though
you walked
the plank
on a pirate ship
sailing rough seas.

Birthday wishes,
each day you are born again.
So, Happy Birthday.

BRICKS

Bricks lay on my heart
stones lay on my soul
nothing could lift the pain
that had grown cold
that had lived
from old, old days
worn to my bone,
cold messages
of bitter memories
laid in shadows I hadn't seen
still don't see
still lay in the dark
where my soul wept
for comfort
that never came,
there I lay too
for comfort that could
have been, had truth
been my mother
instead of sin.

DARKEST CORNER

God speaks
even in the darkest corner
of our mind
even in boring words
so boring
the words sleep
in our thoughts.
God speaks
whispers
sings
cries
evokes us
to be close to Him,
to want to be near
His life
the only life
that has meant
more than life.
God speaks
even when
we do not listen.

EMPTY

Perhaps emptiness
will find you
in solace, peace,
not fear
which will betray
your beauty
your strength
your gifts.

Emptiness
is not the end
it is the beginning,
a place
to be
filled.

EMPTY NEST

No words were formed
in my mind,
only feelings
turned me blind
to recollections of
love you gave
then took,
as I held your face
fleeting like time
unable to stay
my memories
of you lay
at the bottom
of my heart.

FOR OUR TIME AGAIN

By a longing thought
we embrace
always lost to time
us together
in my mind
await our hearts
to meet
when we are gone
from this earth
time no more
will wreak our days
while we bask
in our tears
washing
fleeted hours
as we speak
of no more years
apart.

GOD BROKE THE SILENCE

God broke the silence
with a solitary word
hope changed
every moment after,
darkness became light
the poor became rich
the lost were found
weeping turned to joy,
from shame and misfortune
God found us in our hovels
brought us into mercy
dissolved our concerns
destroyed worry and fear,
He whispered in tiers
of blue skies, His grace
beyond and more
blankets the world
in a solitary word,
love.

GOD TALKS

You look and see
only what you think.
See me, see my life
see my love
it stays with you
even when you
see nothing.

HEAL

If you can
of course you can
you are God
reach down, cleanse
heal the broken heart
mend torn fences,
with torn bodies,
that hold breath to
a strangled world,
send your peace
blaze the trail
clear our way with a
shining, glorious vision
to shame the darkness for
trying to cover the earth.

IN HIS SHADOW

In His shadow
quivering from fear
seeing crumbs,
recalling my mess
regretting my shallow existence
Jesus sits with me and says,
"My love is all you need,
do not worry about deeds
undone and nothingness,
you only need me.
Let me need you,
do not embrace what is gone,
attend this day."
My heart did lift,
His name sat on my lips
as I tried to swallow His truth.
His name I spoke, Jesus,
a moment found light.
He said, "Rise, do not bury yourself,
life is in you, go and sin no more.

JESUS SAID

Jesus said, "I am the way."
But there was nothing to see
so quiet I rest to hear His voice.

A breeze whispered, a tune pulsed,
marched, dragged, swung, stretched, bellowed, hummed
then told me to wait until a door opened.

LEAVE THE GHOSTS

You held my hand
to soothe my longing
peace filled my lungs
then as a snake
you bit, quickly
before I understood
your nature.

Pain and poison
entered my vein
it did kill,
but not to death
it stifled joy,
oppressed goodness,
between us,
what remain
were ashes
of our friendship.

Was that your intent
had you lost your way
could you be found, again
might ashes become ground
might we become friend.

Maybe, in dreams
where all things are right
glory shines and the living God
steps forward to say,
leave the ghosts behind.

MY FOREST DREAM

Into a dim forest,
my dreaming entered
beckoned me to follow
a passage taken by few
stillness motion nocturnal travel
thick darkness lay askew
my world was, but sleeping
resting quiet a loopy fright
into the dense and haunting fog
a wondering dreaming night.

There was nothing to follow
in this vexing brew
of surrounding terror
lay a sooty cool
near my coffin bed
myself could not confide
nor could I run, speak or hide.

Ambushed through night I paced
hoping for a change in fate
my soul jeered into despair
as stone fell on my feet
captive to a tomb we swell
into scrolling coated fear.

Jesus wept in my forest dream
to swim me from this dismal night
none could keep, warm growing cold
until awoken to morning light.

MY HEART HEARS NOTHING

My heart hears nothing
feels only strain
to a schedule,
ordered by me.

Speak
maybe I'll hear,
maybe I'll hear
nothing.

Speak anyhow
so your voice
might seep thru
the cracks of my
congested brain

to let me know
my day
will not be in
vain.

**MY SON AND
SOUL, BURIAL**

Nothing remain
except a muddy sting
no voice heard
no resonating word
only a sleepy, hollow,
wistful mire,
where you sank.

Your name, your name
I wanted to say,
your name
to keep you here.

I called to you,
lifeless and cold,
my heart went too
and fell my soul
for my son,
my joy and vim,
as dirt flew
carried by wind,
my wild, barren, grief
was ground,
until myself
no longer found.

PRAISES TO GOD

Praises to God almighty
who reaches up to heaven
and reaches down to earth
who sings our praises
even in our trenches
of dark despair
yet God sings to us
with joy, to say He is always
with us, we are His,
His life is in us
God embraces our sorrow
coats our fears
whispers in our dreams
you are not lost
God has found you
will never let you go
no matter the dark
you will always,
remain, in His light.

QUAGMIRE

When you looked in my direction,
hope sprung, fresh air blew upon my face
my days no longer dreary, goodness seeped
into every click of every pulse until
together we clung and the clinging stung
together we pushed and shoved until one fell
with none to recover the hurt
no answers, only a battle of pain,
despair, ugly bruises from our war.

What had been my home, turned into a quagmire
of fear, disillusioned trails that sought to destroy,
faith got lost and wandered alone through a dark
forest, scary, trembling, too meek to speak
every day a struggle with wounded scars.

Jesus in His mercy, said, "Do not fear."
In His mercy He touched my hand,
"You are not alone, I go with you to win your heart.
You fight yourself, let me be, all you need,
the quagmire is not for ruin, it is for you to know,
this world is not your home,
do not fear, you are not alone."

QUIET

The quiet of my home
surrounded me with fear,
endeared with tables,
books, chairs, forks and glasses
good memories in my heart,
decapitated with the stroll of hours,
as minutes pushed the day
into tomorrow.
There I rested and
found threats of despair, hovering
like a vulture, waiting to devour
my hope for a good day.
So, Jesus, I sought
to embrace my trembling
to rest in believing
in everlasting.

RANCOUR OF YOU

The rancour
kept pace
with my pounding
head
the wave of pain
kept falling
on my pleading
heart
there would be
no reprieve
no finale
that would complete
this character
building afternoon
so I dropped my head
closed the door to my soul
while your gust
blew threw.

SLEEP DEPRIVED

No voice
No sound
Not even a whisper to say
'You are mine, you belong to me
on sweet dreams you will be carried.'
God left me in the dark,
scraping at the hours, clocks telling me how late
at some point, how early, at some point
I wish I could start my day on no sleep.
I don't think I would last long.
So I listen, to hear your voice,
there was nothing to hear, except my thoughts,
crowded, pushing, stealing my sleeping moments.
So again, I listen, slowly, one by one
my thoughts returned clamoring for attention
until the weariness of thinking wore me out
And I slept.

An hour's sleep is better than none.

STARS HAD FALLEN

Stars had fallen
from the sky
into my lap
where I cried
for wasted days
sleepless nights
headaches, pain
for soggy fights,
for wanting change
that never came
for wanting nothing
but the same,
for time that
pushed me along
when all I wanted,
was to sit, and
look at the stars
in the sky
and pray
they'd stay,
where they are.

THE END

When he departed
hope sprang
to let me know
the finish,
like a seed,
an open door,
the dawn,
a pardon
a chance
to be okay.

THOUGHTS OF YOU

Thoughts of you
in my mind,
like a sunny day.
Where I would,
if I could,
in your memory
stay.

WHEN YOU ARE GONE

When you are gone
sorrow will stay
heavy like mud flows
through my day,
myself I will hardly know
or recognize,
I will wonder why I move at all
I will speak no words
or care for thought
what good will living be
when you're gone,
loss will fill my cup
and drive my years
living still
my lasting fear.

WORDS FROM WALLS

Words from walls
speak louder than
my prayers,
tiny kittens seem
fierce against
my pearls of faith.

Discarded tears
no well can hold
and no draw with years,
of failed attempts,
of being the same,
of misspent time,
and careless claims
of who I am.

In loving grace
Jesus gifts
to bid me rest
not fight or war
be still, my soul
He conquers all.

YOU ARE HEARD

Out of the mire,
the quicksand,
the sinking ship,
from the dry desert
the lonely dark
a place no one
goes or wants to.

Hear my voice
I call to thee.
In your blackest heart,
a truth will spring.
Rise to beauty
grace, hope, love,
embrace the wrong,
embrace my word
you're not forgotten
you are heard.

DM completed a BFA and MFA in dance from New York University, Tisch School of the Arts. Lived in NYC's East Village for 16 years as a modern dancer and worked with many talented choreographers and musicians, including notables as Cindy Lauper, Bertrum Ross, Rachel Harms, XXY Dance/ Music and Pierce Turner. During those years she worked more than 20 'money' jobs for support, including sales in an art gallery, public relations, commercial modeling, floral design and as a dance instructor.

Eventually she long for a backyard and a dog and moved out of New York to the Virginia coast where she adopted a dog, worked for the Governor's School of the Arts, got married and had 2 sons who remain her greatest joy. Also for twelve years worked as a Realtor at Rose and Womble.

DM writes fiction, children stories, non-fiction and poems. She is a creative jack-of-all-trades; interested in everything, but mostly the human dilemma of existence especially late at night when quiet becomes so loud it keeps her awake.

Her father, who passed away in 2010, was a devout Catholic and though she is not practicing, appreciates the Catholic Church, because her father was a loving, kind, funny, fair minded, caring listener. And by some fault, not her own, DM accepted Jesus years ago who stayed in her heart ever since, even when she's not very obedient.

For DM, poems come from words that arrive unexpected, that carry feelings, lift pain, ease anguish, celebrate disappointment, forgave the unforgiveable, burn the wrongs and tell her, everything is okay when left alone with her terrors. Poetry has been a tool to help wade through the quagmire as she chases dreams.

www.ingramcontent.com/pod-product-compliance
Lightning Source LLC
Chambersburg PA
CBHW050822090426
42737CB00022B/3473